TU YOUYOU'S DISCOVERY

FINDING A CURE FOR MALARIA

Songju Ma Daemicke   illustrated by **Lin**

Albert Whitman & Company
Chicago, Illinois

To Professor Tu Youyou and all Chinese
scientists—SMD

You get in life what you have the courage
to ask for.—L

Library of Congress Cataloging-in-Publication data
is on file with the publisher.
Text copyright © 2021 by Songju Ma Daemicke
Illustrations copyright © 2021 by Albert Whitman & Company
Illustrations by Lin
First published in the United States of America in 2021
by Albert Whitman & Company
ISBN 978-0-8075-8111-7 (hardcover)
ISBN 978-0-8075-8110-0 (ebook)

Printed in China
10 9 8 7 6 5 4 3 2 1 WKT 26 25 24 23 22 21

Design by Valerie Hernández

For more information about Albert Whitman & Company,
visit our website at www.albertwhitman.com.

In 1969, people all across the world were sick. Malaria, a life-threatening disease carried by mosquitoes, was spreading quickly and seemed resistant to all known treatments.

Reading the news in her Beijing apartment, Tu Youyou was distressed. Many people were suffering, and she had wanted to help save lives since she was a child.

Though most girls in 1930s China didn't go to school, Youyou's parents valued education, and sent her along with her brothers.

Curious Youyou loved her classes, especially science. But at the age of fifteen, she became severely ill with tuberculosis, a serious lung disease, and she had to stop going to school.

After several bedridden months, Youyou woke up in a strange room, her mother clasping her hands. Youyou's throat was raw and red, but she smiled weakly. She could breathe again! Antibiotics, prescribed by her doctor, had saved her life.

Youyou began to recover but was still too weak to leave her home. Over the next two years, her mother's herb soups slowly nursed her back to full strength.

As she healed, she thought about how different kinds of medicine, both modern and traditional, had helped her.

She decided she wanted to study science and save lives, just as her life had been saved.

Following her dream, Youyou studied medicine at Peking University and then in 1955 became a researcher at the China Academy of Traditional Chinese Medicine in Beijing.

Then in 1969, when malaria began sweeping the world, Youyou knew it was her time to help. Because of her background, the academy chose her to start a research group. Their only goal was to find a cure to this deadly disease.

After spending time studying many traditional Chinese medicine books, Youyou began traveling to Chinese provinces where malaria had spread widely.

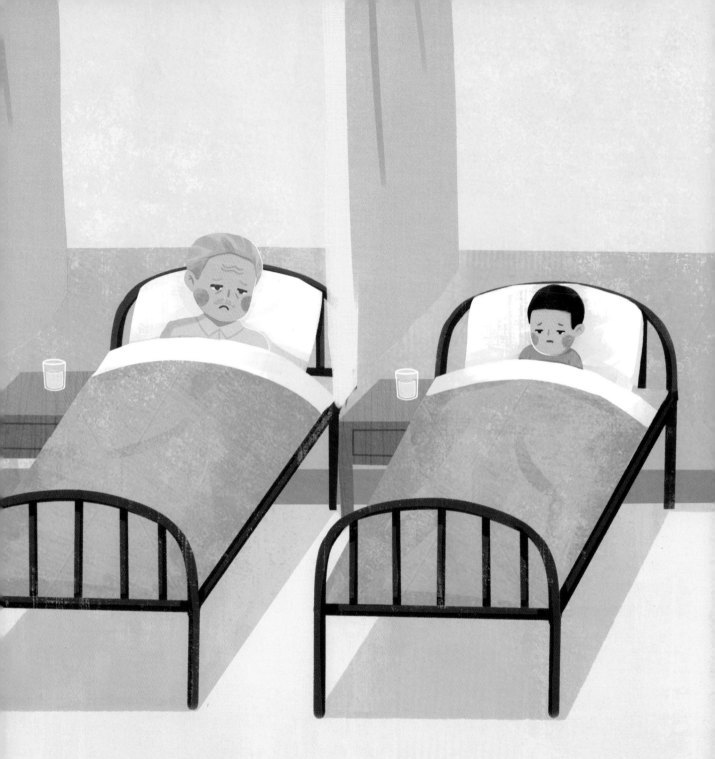

At a clinic in Hainan, Youyou witnessed patients of all ages shivering and sweating. Chloroquine, a Western malaria medicine, hadn't helped. She asked the patients questions about their symptoms and experiences.

One farmer's story sprouted hope in Youyou. Trembling with a high fever, he had seen some qinghao, a grassy plant, near his home. He'd remembered an old folk saying that recommended qinghao as a fever medicine, so he'd pulled and eaten several handfuls of the plant. The next day, his fever had gone away.

Excited, Youyou dug up some qinghao,
which in English is called sweet wormwood.

Back at her lab, Youyou and her team washed
and cut the plants into pieces, soaked them in water
for hours, then boiled, filtered, and condensed them
into a thick liquid.

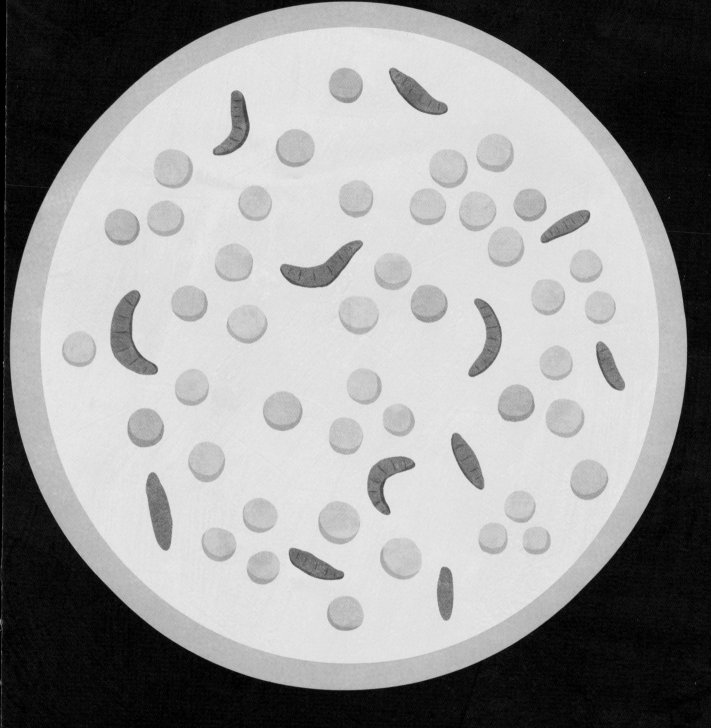

But when they tested it against the disease, the malaria parasites just kept wriggling under the microscope. Why hadn't it worked? Youyou was determined to keep experimenting.

Her lab couldn't afford expensive equipment. The team worked in rooms without fans or air-conditioning. They opened windows and wore face masks to protect themselves from harmful chemicals.

They tested *hundreds* of herbs and compounds through trial and error.

Pepper wasn't strong enough.

Alum, a type of salt, was poisonous.

Changshan, a common blue flower, caused vomiting.

The project seemed to be at a dead end.

After thinking about all their experiments that hadn't worked,
Youyou's team refocused on qinghao, the most popular folk remedy.

Late one night, Youyou couldn't sleep. She pulled out her well-read family copy of *A Handbook of Prescriptions for Emergencies*, an ancient Chinese remedy book. Youyou reread the "qinghao remedy":

青蒿一握, 以水二升渍, 绞取汁, 尽服之。

"A handful of qinghao immersed in two liters of water, wring out the juice and drink it all."

Almost all herb preparations in the lab used a boiling process, but this remedy didn't mention boiling, only soaking in water. Could heat have destroyed the parts of qinghao that could heal?

The next morning, Youyou rushed to her lab and redesigned the experiments using lower temperatures. Then, more extracting, more testing, more analyzing, more adjusting.

Still, the experiments kept failing—more than one hundred with no success.

Some male researchers began to question Youyou's leadership and doubt the direction of her research. Western countries with advanced technologies hadn't found a cure. Was using herbal medicine to cure malaria an impossible goal?

But Youyou was stubborn. Her faith in traditional Chinese medicine was unshakable. She kept working and testing.
Then something incredible happened.

After 190 unsuccessful experiments, the test result of sample 191 stunned the team. The qinghao extract prepared at a temperature of only 94 degrees Fahrenheit had killed the parasites completely!

After the successful test of the sweet wormwood extract, the team named the medicine artemisinin, or qinghaosu (青蒿素) in Chinese. Qinghao, a plant used across 2,000 years of Chinese medicine to treat fevers, had been rediscovered as a cure for malaria in 1971.

Youyou signed her team's name instead of her own on the initial published research papers. Years later, other scientists finally realized how involved she had been in the discovery. It was Youyou who first brought the qinghao plant to the project, started testing at lower temperatures, and carried out the first clinical trial on humans.

In 2015 Tu Youyou received the Nobel Prize in Medicine, making her the first Chinese woman to win a Nobel Prize of any kind. Standing in the magnificent Stockholm Concert Hall to accept this prestigious award, Youyou felt immense joy. She had saved millions of lives.

Humbly, yet proudly, Youyou said, "Artemisinin (is) a gift
from traditional Chinese medicine to the world."

TIMELINE

1930 Tu Youyou is born on December 30 in Ningbo, in the Zhejiang Province of China. Her father named her "Youyou" after a poem in *Shijing,* a famous book of Chinese poetry.

1946 Tu Youyou falls sick with tuberculosis and does not fully recover for two years.

1955 Tu Youyou graduates with a BA in pharmaceutical science from Peking University and works as researcher at the China Academy of Traditional Chinese Medicine in Beijing.

1963 Tu Youyou marries Li Tingzhao, a classmate from high school.

1965 Their first daughter, Li Ming, is born.

1967 The Cultural Revolution, a political movement that did not support traditional Chinese or Western cultures, begins. Many experienced scientists who had connections to those cultures were sent to "reeducation" schools, including Youyou's husband.

1968 Their second daughter, Li Jun, is born.

1969 On January 21, Tu Youyou starts an antimalarial research group at the China Academy of Traditional Chinese Medicine and joins Project 523, a top secret government project that includes more than 2,000 researchers.

1971 In September, Tu Youyou's team refocuses their research on the sweet wormwood plant.

1971 Experiment 191 is successful on October 4.

1972 Tu Youyou's team conducts the first clinical trial of the qinghao extract in August. Tu Youyou's husband is assigned to work at a reeducation school in Yunnan Province, as a part of the Cultural Revolution. Youyou sends her oldest daughter to a boarding school and her youngest daughter to live with her parents in Ningbo.

1972 Sweet wormwood extract crystal, called artemisinin, is produced for the first time on November 8th.

1970s Late in the decade, Tu Youyou and her family are reunited after many years apart.

1986 Artemisinin is officially approved as a new medication.

2015 Tu Youyou is awarded the Nobel Prize in Medicine in October.

AUTHOR'S NOTE

Even though Tu Youyou carried out the first clinical trials for artemisinin in 1972, it took fourteen more years for the medicine to be approved by the Chinese government and start being used worldwide. Malaria still affects countries in Africa, Southeast Asia, the Eastern Mediterranean, and the Western Pacific, but from 2000-2015, the rate of new malaria cases declined globally by an estimated 37 percent, and the mortality rate fell by 60 percent. By 2013 more than 90 percent of affected African countries had adopted artemisinin-based therapies as their primary treatment. According to Dr. Margaret Chan, former director general of the World Health Organization, "Between 2001 and 2015, a cumulative total of 6.8 million lives were saved."

TU YOUYOU AND THE SCIENTIFIC METHOD

Tu Youyou's search for a cure for malaria is a shining example of the scientific method at work. The scientific method consists of six steps:

1. Scientists must ask a question. In this story, Youyou and many others questioned how they could cure malaria.

2. Scientists must do background research. Youyou spent three months studying traditional Chinese medical books and collected 640 folk remedies before she began experimenting.

3. Scientists must make a hypothesis. A hypothesis is an educated guess about what might answer the main question. Tu Youyou hypothesized that one herb should be able to treat malaria effectively and that it might be found in traditional Chinese medicine.

4. Scientists begin experimenting and collecting data. Youyou's team designed experiments to extract medicinal components from herbs, test the extract against malaria parasites, and record the results.

5. Scientists analyze the data and draw conclusions. Each time they tested an herb, Youyou's team analyzed the results to determine whether or not it had affected the malaria parasites. When the results were not successful, the team repeated steps four and five until they found a successful result.

6. Finally, scientists communicate the results. Youyou's team shared their results, which allowed for clinical trials to begin and the eventual mass production of the life-saving artemisinin.

SELECTED BIBLIOGRAPHY

Fact Sheet: World Malaria Report 2015. World Health Organization, 2015.

Liu, Liping. *Tu Youyou: China's First Nobel Prize Winning Female Scientist.* London: ACA, 2016.

Rao, Yi, and Daqing Zhang. *Tu Youyou and the Discovery of Artemisinin: 2015 Nobel Laureate in Physiology or Medicine.* Singapore: World Scientific, 2016.

Zhang, Wenhu. *Tu Youyou's Journey in the Search for Artemisinin.* Singapore: World Scientific, 2018.